# LIVING ADVENTUROUSLY

## Questions and Answers

Alastair Humphreys

Name:

In case of loss, please return to:

Reward:

# INTRODUCTION

Once upon a time, I climbed onto my bike, waved goodbye to my Mum and Dad and set off to try to cycle around the world. I was 24 years old.

Since then I have crossed continents, oceans and deserts in pursuit of adventure. But my perception of adventure has changed a great deal since I first traded the green hills of Yorkshire for the open road.

Everyone's definition of living adventurously is unique. I love that. It could be crossing a desert or cross-dressing, running a marathon or running a non-profit. And it also changes over time, as our lives and circumstances change. These days my adventures and microadventures need to fit in around the happy chaos of raising a family.

Since pedalling away from home all those years ago, my adventures have evolved from fun to machismo to curiosity to scaring myself to seizing the moment. I began to understand that if I wished to continue living adventurously, then I should not just repeat the same types of expedition I was familiar with. In its own way, they were my comfort zone, my routine and rut. Wondering what direction my life might go in next, I decided to get back on my bike and ask a range of different people what living adventurously means to them.

I learned that you can live adventurously anywhere: in your office or home as well as in the hills. You don't have to be rich or fit or young or talented. Living adventurously is merely the attitude you charge at life with. And anyone can choose their attitude. It is about being eager to look differently at things, to be bold and risk looking a fool. It invites us to stretch ourselves mentally, physically or culturally. To attempt fresh challenges. To accept the risk of failure in exchange for the enticing sense of surprised satisfaction upon completion.

Living adventurously is not about being lucky enough to have an adventure of a lifetime one day. Instead, it is a choice to live a more adventurous life every day. You can begin living more adventurously right now, without needing to spend a penny.

Though I am currently exiled down in the south of England, I grew up in God's own county. Like most of our tribe, I identify proudly and loudly as a Yorkshireman. But I was aware that there was loads of my home county that I had never seen. This prompted me to spend a month cycling around Yorkshire, wild camping and following my nose along the way. It was a wonderful experience.

Eventually, and reluctantly, came the final miles of the journey. I circled back towards my childhood home, down into the dales and villages that I knew so well. I cycled the bridleways where I first dabbled with off-road riding as a boy. I passed the pub where I used to work in, then my old school. The memories lay thick all around me. Finally I pedalled up to the house I grew up in, the home where my parents still live today. This small adventure ended where my first big adventure had begun.

I had been curious whether I could have a genuine 'travel' experience and a memorable journey without flying half way around the world. I wanted to see whether one small region could hold my attention if I tried to really pay attention. Could a mere month pedalling through my home county in any way replicate the years I spent cycling across continent after continent? The answer to all these questions was a resounding 'Yes'. Cycling around Yorkshire was one of the most intriguing, varied, rewarding and enjoyable journeys of my life.

But the best part of the trip, by a long way, was the opportunity to learn from so many ordinary people who are choosing to live extra-ordinary lives. I met students and parents and pensioners. Poets, artists, athletes, teachers. Someone who earns a living from making fancy sandcastles. Another whose family castle has been passed down for 800 years. I met a self-confessed lazy Michelin chef and a woman midway through running 100 barefoot marathons. I interviewed a gold medal Paralympian cyclist, a couple who had cycled the world together, and a retired lady who takes old, homebound, lonely folk out on a modified electric bicycle for a taste of freedom, adventure and 'feeling the wind in their hair' once again. All of these people were kind enough to sit down with me to talk about their slant on living a curious, adventurous, fulfilled life. Turning those chats into a podcast has been one of my favourite projects.

To help steer the conversations, I had a deck of playing cards on which I'd written questions about finding a balance between work and play, the barriers that stop us doing what we dream of, how we overcome fears, and where you sit on a scale of weirdness from 1 to 10. The questions were a mixture of my own musings about life, a few goodies borrowed from other interviews, and crowd-sourced suggestions from Twitter. Asking very different people an assortment of similar questions generated a fascinating range of answers. The cards were usually my favourite part of the interview.

My podcast listeners often ask about the cards and are interested in having a go at answering them. And so here are the questions from the cards, laid out in a simple notebook. Answer each one thoroughly and you will be well on the way to writing the backstory to your autobiography as well as planning the next decade of your life! I hope the questions help you figure out your own path towards living a little more adventurously every day, as they have done for me.

You can, of course, use this notebook however you wish, whether as kindling, expedition loo roll or to prop up a wobbly pub table. My suggestion though would be that you answer the questions with written thoughts rather than just skimming them in your head. Better still, discuss them out loud with your family, friends or class while sitting around a dinner table, a campfire, or a hilltop. I noticed during my podcast interviews the shift in people's expressions between reading a question quietly, articulating their thoughts to me, and then flowing into whatever surprising conversation that led to.

So get thinking, get your pen out, get outside, get planning. If you would like to share your scribblings you could post them online using the #LivingAdventurously hashtag or challenge your friends to answer them.

And please do dip into the Living Adventurously interviews on your podcast app or via www.alastairhumphreys.com/podcasts

Would you like to live more adventurously? I know that I certainly would.

Alastair Humphreys

# LIVING ADVENTUROUSLY

Questions and Answers

What does 'living adventurously' mean to you? Has that definition changed with time? What did it mean to you as a child?

What is a good decision you have made in life? What can that teach me about making decisions?

What story would you put on the front page of the newspaper?

What would you say to someone who told you that your life was becoming less adventurous?

Did anyone ever warn you against being adventurous? How did it feel? How does it feel now?

How could you be happier?

---

What is an absurd thing that you love?

---

Why do you not act when you know what to do?

Are you sacrificing your present happiness for the sake of a happier future, or the other way round?

What is the question that you are afraid to ask?

What is stopping you from living more adventurously?

On a scale of 1 to 10, how weird are you?

---

Should I choose security or what makes my heart sing? Tell me about a time of joy or of uncertainty.

---

---

Tell me about trying to live a full, adventurous life and still also fulfil your responsibilities.

---

What are you doing at times you feel that you are being a good parent / partner / spouse / sibling / friend?

---

Tell me about the last time you
climbed a tree or swam in a river
or watched the sun set from
a hilltop.

---

What book should I read to make myself more wild, bold, and curious?

Tell me how you find
a balance between work, play,
money and family.

---

Do you wish you had more freedom?

---

How would your life be different if you were a millionaire?

---

If you could pause everything and spend a year doing whatever you wanted, what would you do?

---

---

Tell me the story of something you regret.

---

What won't you be able to do in ten years' time that you can do now?

---

Do you need to earn money or do you want to earn money?

---

---

What is the biggest question you would like to answer in your own life?

---

Do you want to live more adventurously? If so, why?

What is the right balance between being selfish vs selfless?

---

What is your favourite failure in life? Why was it important?

---

---

Tell me about making the most out of life.

---

If you could live life over, what would you do differently?

---

What advice would you offer to someone who has the same big barriers that are in your head and stop you getting on with things?

---

Who was the most adventurous grown-up you knew when you were a child?

# What is Enough?

---

If you could only work two hours per week in your business, what would you do?

---

In the last five years, what new belief, behaviour or habit has most improved your life?

Do you think you will manage to become the person you want to be?

If you had one extra hour, every day, all to yourself, how would you spend it?

Within reason we can do anything. But we cannot do everything. How do you choose how to spend your energy and time?

What three things do you need to do to live a life of purpose?

Are you doing what you love?

What purchase of £100 or less has most positively impacted your life recently?

---

If you could magically change one thing in your life, what would it be?

---

Who do you want to remember you (and how) when you are dead?

What’s holding you back?
Why haven’t you already begun?

What are you willing to sacrifice for ambition?

What small thing do you
do regularly which greatly improves
your life?

Can you share an
example of trying to find a balance
between contentment and self-improvement?

What advice can you give me
so that I look back on my life with
satisfaction rather than regrets?

---

If you asked your childhood self who you thought you would become, would you measure up? What three things would your younger self be proud of?

---

---

Stick or Twist. In general, my life is comfortable and happy. Should I risk a new challenge and make big changes or settle for what I have?

---

## What are you proud of?

## What do you want to be when you grow up?

Can you share an example of what the word ‘Home’ means to you?

What would the 80-year-old version of yourself advise you to do?

---

Ask me a hard question. (What hard questions would you like to ask other people?)

---

What were the two happiest periods of your life?

---

What did you think that being aged X was going to be like? What is it actually like?

---

What would a life spent living adventurously look like to you?

- Are you doing what you love?
- Are you sacrificing your present happiness for the sake of a happier future, or the other way round?
- Ask me a hard question. (What hard questions would you like to ask other people?)
- Can you share an example of trying to find a balance between contentment and self-improvement?
- Can you share an example of what the word 'Home' means to you?
- Did anyone ever warn you against being adventurous? How did it feel? How does it feel now?
- Do you need to earn money or do you want to earn money?
- Do you think you will manage to become the person you want to be?
- Do you want to live more adventurously? If so, why?
- Do you wish you had more freedom?
- How could you be happier?
- How would your life be different if you were a millionaire?
- If you asked your childhood self who you thought you would become, would you measure up? What three things would your younger self be proud of?
- If you could live life over, what would you do differently?
- If you could magically change one thing in your life, what would it be?
- If you could only work two hours per week on your business, what would you do?
- If you could pause everything and spend a year doing whatever you wanted, what would you do?
- If you had one extra hour, every day, all to yourself, how would you spend it?
- In the last five years, what new belief, behaviour or habit has most improved your life?
- On a scale of 1 to 10, how weird are you?
- Should I choose security or what makes my heart sing? Tell me about a time of joy or of uncertainty.

- Stick or Twist. In general, my life is comfortable and happy. Should I risk a new challenge and make big changes or settle for what I have?
- Tell me about making the most out of life.
- Tell me about the last time you climbed a tree or swam in a river or watched the sun set from a hilltop.
- Tell me about trying to live a full, adventurous life and still also fulfil your responsibilities.
- Tell me how you find a balance between work, play, money and family.
- Tell me the story of something you regret.
- What advice can you give me so that I look back on my life with satisfaction rather than regrets?
- What advice would you offer to someone who has the same big barriers that are in your head and stop you getting on with things?
- What are you doing at times you feel that you are being a good parent / partner / spouse / sibling / friend?
- What are you proud of?
- What are you willing to sacrifice for ambition?
- What book should I read to make myself more wild, bold, and curious?
- What did you think that being aged X was going to be like? What is it actually like?
- What do you want to be when you grow up?
- What does 'living adventurously' mean to you? Has that definition changed with time? What did it mean to you as a child?
- What is a good decision you have made in life? What can that teach me about making decisions?
- What is an absurd thing that you love?
- What is Enough?
- What is stopping you from living more adventurously?
- What is the biggest question you would like to answer in your own life?
- What is the question that you are afraid to ask?
- What is the right balance between being selfish vs selfless?

- What is your favourite failure in life? Why was it important?
- What purchase of £100 or less has most positively impacted your life recently?
- What small thing do you do regularly which greatly improves your life?
- What story would you put on the front page of the newspaper?
- What three things do you need to do to live a life of purpose?
- What were the two happiest periods of your life?
- What won't you be able to do in ten years' time that you can do now?
- What would a life spent living adventurously look like to you?
- What would the 80-year-old version of yourself advise you to do?
- What would you say to someone who told you that your life was becoming less adventurous?
- What's holding you back? Why haven't you already begun?
- Who do you want to remember you (and how) when you are dead?
- Who was the most adventurous grown-up you knew when you were a child?
- Why do you not act when you know what to do?
- Within reason we can do anything. But we cannot do everything. How do you choose how to spend your energy and time?

## ABOUT THE AUTHOR

Alastair Humphreys is a British Adventurer and Author. He spent over 4 years cycling round the world, a journey of 46,000 miles through 60 countries and 5 continents.

Alastair has also walked across southern India, rowed across the Atlantic Ocean, run six marathons through the Sahara desert, completed a crossing of Iceland, busked through Spain and participated in an expedition in the Arctic, close to the magnetic North Pole. He has trekked 1000 miles across the Empty Quarter desert and 120 miles round the M25 – one of his pioneering microadventures. Alastair was named as one of National Geographic's Adventurers of the year for 2012. He has written 13 books, including several for children.

**Podcasts by Alastair Humphreys** - available on your podcast app or www.alastairhumphreys.com/podcasts

- Living Adventurously
- The Doorstep Mile
- There Are Other Rivers

**Free email newsletters by Alastair Humphreys** - available at www.alastairhumphreys.com/newsletters

- Shouting from the Shed
- The Doorstep Mile
- The Working Adventurer

## OTHER STUFF:

Instagram / Twitter: @al_humphreys

YouTube / Facebook: Alastair Humphreys

Photos of the podcast guests: https://bit.ly/3dQiLAI

Photos from my Yorkshire adventure: https://bit.ly/3dM3fWl

## THANK YOU:

Book Design: Kim Farrall and Sally Evans // www.somewhereoffgrid.com // @somewhereoffgrid

Cover Design: Matty Waudby // www.mattywaudby.com // @getwildmatty

Thank you to everyone I interviewed for sharing your conversation, company, humour, wisdom, coffee, tea, beer, food and homes.

Printed in Great Britain
by Amazon